I0469869

YOUR BUSINESS, YOUR RETIREMENT

Halton Retirement Study – 2015

Brian Weatherdon

MA, CFP, CLU, CPCA, CRC, MDRT.
brian@sovereignwealth.ca
905-637-3500 x 223

Copyright © 2015 Brian Weatherdon

ISBN 978-1516862801

Note: views expressed are those of the author alone and do not necessarily reflect the financial firms and product manufacturers he represents, or professional associations with which he is associated.

Other books by this author:
A Lifetime of Wealth – And How Not To Lose It (2013)
Protecting Life, Loved Ones, and Future Dreams (2013)

Educational Website and additional resources:
www.GuaranteedIncome4Life.ca

Front cover-photo: special thanks to Gillian Sheldon

1

CONTENTS

INTRODUCTION

Business and lifestyle goals for retirement intersect vividly. Whether the future appears sunny or stormy depends on our preparation in ways we might never have considered. If we don't get this right, many will suffer losses that could earlier have been avoided – diminishing their financial security and retirement lifestyles.

Who stands to lose? Those who own, manage, or are employed in business today. Also our families. Ultimately also our estates. Community also loses when business shuts the doors or limps ahead on an old and worn-out vision. If we only herald start-ups and move-ins, we risk losing out on the potential renewal and rescaling of existing businesses …with resulting loss, especially to age-50+ professionals, owners, and staff, whose nest eggs are severely threatened.

In 2013, I wrote <u>A Lifetime of Wealth – and How Not To Lose It</u>. Chapter 2 offers key topics of transition planning in business (and life) and how key professionals can align as a "stewardship team" to optimize exit strategies and sustain community business.

Today, I'm offering you independent research alongside other valuable studies and resources. Do you have time to pore through the studies published by McKinsey & Company, Ipsos Reid, Brondesbury Group, and others? Or have you read and reflected on Dr. Richard Johnson's practical insights published in 2001 and 2006 as <u>The New Retirement, Discovering Your Dream</u> and <u>What Color is your Retirement?</u> In this paper, we will distill and gather valuable insights from these wider works in support of Your Business, Your Retirement.

My own surveys and interviews align with key areas of Dr. Johnson's clinical experience and teaching on retirement planning and adult development. To this, I sharpen our focus on the role of business and career as a prime area in which we express our personal "value" and the platform from which we may leap – *safely or not* – into a lengthy retirement.

As a matter of procedure, you could say I'm turning "polls" upside down. What I mean is this: Imagine you're flying commercially over the Rockies near Banff National Park in Alberta.

Looking down you see a two-dimensional relief, obscuring all the detailed grandeur and magnificence of these mountains. But now imagine standing at the top of Sulphur Mountain, slowly turning 360° to catch the breathlessly unspeakable beauty of the surrounding mountains and valleys, the Bow River Valley surging eastward, eagles soaring *below you!*, and perhaps a rainbow, not overhead but down in the valley below. A little lower than the angels we stand amid the thrust and pull of life and business, *not*

asking what 2,000 or 12,000 people say, but asking what YOU say, thus making this study a very personal journey for each of us.

It's about you!   Surveys offer the map but miss the location. Your experience and perspective are borne of your personal history, challenges, dreams and desires. What's the exact landscape in your life today? What concerns, strengths, supports, and outcomes are most vital and relevant for you right now? If we can capture the wider data and allow you a personal 360° of your career, business, relationships, leisure, lifestyle and desired future, what could this open for you?

Also for others! This study goes beyond the creative stress of our own business and retirement. Successful transitions for our generation also require safe horizons for existing staff, all our families, and sustaining value for wider community.

As we'll soon see, the present study will address personal values and experiences, beliefs and behaviours that may: **(i)** keep us active in a current enterprise, **(ii)** move us toward full retirement, or **(iii)** fuel our "new retirement" enterprises.

We'll touch on the <u>five primary purposes of work</u> (time, money, purpose, identity, social) and how we can express "self" and personal destiny beyond career and business. We'll look ahead to experiences that deepen and expand the sense of "awe" and gratitude in life. Where events seem to block progress, we'll explore how to unlock this journey to create the future we truly seek.

> If 40% of businesses are due to sell or transition over the next
> five years, how many here represent our friends and colleagues?
> Is a business owner delaying necessary next steps to prepare
> the way? Lack of preparation suggests risk of illness or death,
> changing markets, failing cash flows, lack of adapting, even
> leaving things until no value is left. Who loses? Employers,
> employees, families, and futures, indeed a whole community.

A few stories can help set the scene before we dive into this survey and the personal interviews in which many readers contributed. In each page here keep your internal dialogue as personal as possible – not about others so much as about yourself and those closest to you.

Sue and Jack wanted more time away from business and to increase their travels. Their process was to arrange an employee-succession. Results were soon plagued by contention among the staff with the result that this business fell off the map. Sale value: zero. Family value: zero. Staff had to seek new jobs. Community lost a tax-paying business.

Dave was enjoying the wave's crest ten years ago. At 60 with high energy, that was "too soon to retire". He confesses now, he has wanted to retire since 2007. Family reasons too are pulling him to leave. But business has dropped; value is down 75%. No buyers, no interest. Fortunately staff is faithful but any landmine to the owner could devastate his team members.

Val and Lee want to retire in 5 years. They've expanded their products and have a strong sales team – but none are positioned for ownership. Costs have risen, currency is a wildcard, and profitability per product ranges 5% to near 50%. Past consultants have generally resulted in a jaded view of outside help. A more recent consulting engagement has increased clarity about the company's vision and levers to success. Result is increasing margins and business valuation, suited to a greater range of potential acquirers.

Jan and Sue describe their professional services. Neither expected to sell this business …but, on the other hand, staff are taking an increasing share of responsibilities when Jan and Sue are away so perhaps a buyer could indeed walk into this business and continue its service and growth. Sue says, "Neither of us can quit working. We're here another ten years at least!" Jan adds. "People go downhill when they retire." But you might wonder if this couple has actually designed their own "pre-retirement" …a "new retirement" that can fit many in today's boomer generation.

Explore and share this further. I hope our words and conversations will ripple forward into the days and seasons ahead, confirming your personal vision and aspirations for retirement …for ourselves and our families, staff and their families, and the expanding value of business in sustaining our growing communities.

"80% of all businesses are family-owned and/or operated. … Family businesses have additional dynamics that add significant competitive advantages to the economy. Attributes of family businesses include greater roles in local communities, higher emphasis on customer loyalty, and a culture of shared values. An ageing entrepreneurial sector, therefore, gives rise to significant risks… Succession… from one entrepreneur to the next, and the tools that facilitate this transition, should be at the forefront of economic and social policy." CFIB June 2005 "Succession Can Breed Success – SME Succession and Canada's Economic Prosperity"

"Like many owners of a privately-owned business, you may be thinking about your transition to the next stage of your life. … Whether you are on the doorstep of retirement or looking into the future … the choices are not often clear, sometimes conflicting, and almost always stressful. …decisions you make will affect the future of the business, your customers, your employees and … your family." Succession Planning Toolkit for Business Owners – leveraging your life's work. CICA, 2006.

QUESTION #1: To ensure Money for Retirement I most likely:

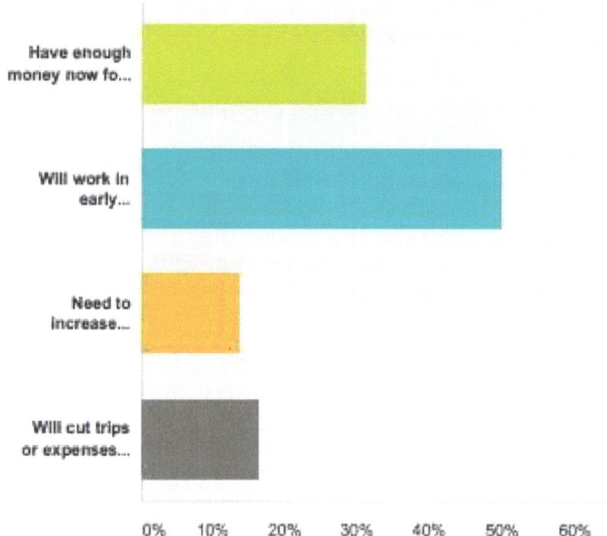

33% of respondents feel money is not an issue at all. 31% offered that they already have enough for all they need or want, and 2% skipped the question. Here too is the family-business where an aging parent remains at the helm while next-generation successors are taking up the reins. So let's continue …

50% of us intend to work in early retirement ...not surprising since people in business often maintain their career longer than most employees would do. However the rationale is striking: **"Will work in early retirement to earn extra money."** Besides other rewards of working, gaining sufficient wealth to avoid worry causes many today to delay retiring from business.

13% are concluding (at this age!) they need to increase investment risk in the hope of augmenting their savings. Results can go either way – win or lose – a tough risk in the five years before or after retirement. Business owners may be either very conservative or aggressive with investments outside their business. The problem with being conservative today is that investments may never grow. And being overly aggressive, losses may never be recovered. High-risk behaviour (conservative or aggressive) can widen the gap – deplete savings – unless there is a strong focus on your "life income mandates". *(See picture of the "Gap" in Q.8)*

16% say they will cut trips or expenses now, in order to boost retirement savings. Link this

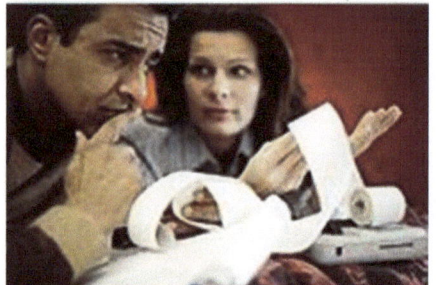

with our discussion in Q.7 on strategies to boost savings now by 5% or in the future by 5-10%. *Some say, "We may not have tomorrow, so enjoy life and make memories today!" Indeed I realize this each time I deliver the death benefit for someone's life insurance.* 16% aren't saying they want to live on a shoestring budget now, but they're willing to cut costs today in order to expand and preserve the lifestyle and memories they want to enjoy in retirement.

An astonishing 67% of colleagues who own and/or manage businesses in our region are less than confident in their financial wellbeing for retirement. Insufficient savings and ongoing costs could be the problem: see Q.7. Or they're stymied by not seeing a clear and abundant plan for their future: see Q.8. So now they're prepared to keep working, increase risks, cut expenses, postpone traveling and lifestyle today …in order to keep building wealth for a comfortable and fulfilling retirement. Let's continue with these questions and see if we can't lighten the load and offer a more cheery, encouraging view of our future wellbeing.

Personal Perspective. What is your take on this? How would you answer this question today? If you were having a private round-table with your most trusted advisors what areas would you discuss? Are you already confident in your financial resources, and if so what risks could arise that would abruptly steal some of that value out of your hands? Risks known as the "4Ds" are death, disability, disease, and departure: if such were to hit someone in your home or business what could be the impact and who would it touch over time?

Other risks are unique to business, or investments. What could go wrong, and therefore what prior actions (now) would help secure the journey? …and, if "worry" is the issue, is there an actual shortfall or just the perception and fear of shortfall: some people delay retiring needlessly as a Certified Financial Plan (see Q.8) could prove they have plenty and to spare.

I've done this survey with different groups and demographics. I had expected to find far more financial confidence among business owners/managers, but I was wrong. Two-thirds feel substantially short of savings to secure retirement …or as we'll see later, many have never seen a certified plan (see Q.8) that helps them conscientiously secure their future goals with the financial resources they have in hand.

Business owners may "fail to plan financially to leave their business, often because they need to continue to invest in the business at the expense of their retirement savings and because of their uncertainty about the timing of their departure. Others find their retirement nest egg is tied up in the equity that they have in their business." Succession Planning Toolkit for Business Owners – leveraging your life's work. CICA, 2006.

QUESTION #2: To expand Life's Purpose & Significance in Retirement I may: *(select one or more)*

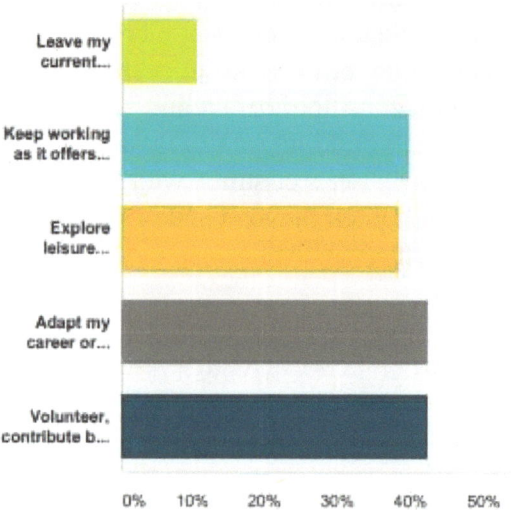

Work isn't all about money. When winter storms block the region and your neighbour is stuck, you'll be one of the first to help. Not for money but for the great feelings of friendship, purpose, significance. We want to feel that our life is important to others, that we can make our world a better place (locally and globally).

Without "purpose" we're dead. Like George Eastman, founder of Kodak. Shortly after retiring he left a note, "My life is over, why wait?" It was as blunt and quick as that.

40% of our business colleagues say they will "Keep working as it offers purpose and something to do". The idea of retirement can seem a tragic waste if our lively sense of "purpose" comes from our career and business. Is this a clue to why some delay retiring, sale or succession of business? They could point to George Eastman and say, "Look, he would have chosen to keep living if he hadn't retired!" Without something purposeful to do, we'd shy from anything that looks like a black hole.

10% offer to "Leave my current role a year or two sooner" because already they are feeling starved and needing something new. Following are some of the areas they plan to expand.

42% say they will adapt current roles to a next-stage and new-purpose. This includes someone who moves into consulting or joins the business faculty at a nearby university. It includes migrating key responsibilities to a next generation (staff and/or family) while moving into mentorship. Angel-investing, business consulting, CEO-for-hire, are a few of the many ways we can express our passion to regain and enlarge "purpose."

42% also aim to "Volunteer, contribute by helping others". Countless are the ways! Rotary, Community Foundations, faith groups, and other avenues of helping our neighbours: if we've done this a bit already, it can become a compelling purpose and engagement over the years ahead. One business owner protests though, saying: "No, why add more responsibility!" Another points to the "good for everyone" simply by continuing in his business. Others say they've never had time, so learning how and where to volunteer can channel their experience in valuable new ways.

38% identify "leisure" as an area of expanding their purpose and significance. Keep this in mind over the next two questions, for leisure certainly doesn't mean sitting around. One professional sees her "new-retirement" as organizing small-group tours to build clinics and schools in vulnerable communities elsewhere in the world. This combines her leisure and purpose. Another person, while reducing his career, has been coaching basketball among young men in a difficult neighbourhood. If we were to brainstorm 50 ideas – even 20 – what would appear in our list of creative leisure that expands our life purpose and significance?

Personal Perspective. Recall how Abraham Maslow described our progress in life, from satisfying basic needs to "self-actualization." Without purpose we are dead. With yesterday's purpose we grow dissatisfied and feel there must be more! To stay alive the shark must always be moving forward, not because sharks are nasty but because this is the metaphor for all life. To feel truly alive and vital, we tend to expand our interests and cultivate new ways of engaging in our world. This can certainly fit into our sense of work, or new-retirement careers (paid or volunteer) including innumerable kinds of leisure. Imagine doing your personal 360° on the highest mountain …or in a serene solitary river valley, what would you want to say to yourself about your life, your feeling of purpose, and where business, career, and retirement fit into your maximum enjoyment and success?

"…business owners may delay retirement because they are emotionally attached to their business. Again, this is not a surprise. They have built a business, nurtured it through good and bad, and it can be difficult to put all of that behind to start a new life." The Estate Planning Toolkit for Business Owners. CICA 2009.

QUESTION #3: Leisure to me especially means:

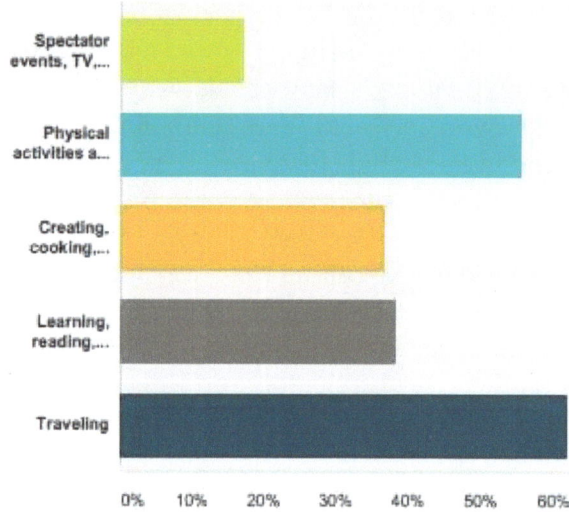

We wouldn't limit leisure to just one choice, so we asked for people's top two selections. Interestingly we are especially engaged with choices that are active and creative. Lowest support overall are the **17%** who put TV, watching sports, spectator events among their two choices.

By the way, let's pose a definition that **"leisure"** is something that is innately diversionary and refreshing from our normal course of duties. If you ponder it, this is both brief and profound. Saying more would be commentary, but I welcome your thoughts as we can expand what leisure means for you.

"Traveling" is the absolute winner showing 62%. In other discussions I know it also matters where and how one will be traveling. Critical of course is the cost. This reminds us of Q.1 as 50% say they'll keep working to earn more money. Also Q.6 where 61% say their greatest

anxiety is not having enough money. What budget will allow you to fulfil this top priority? Enough to hike the Bruce Trail or the Camino Santiago? Enough to cruise from Vancouver to the Alaska Ice Fields or from Amsterdam to Austria? Or all of the above? What dreams? …what costs? And if we build this lifestyle into your "retirement and financial planning" would it set you free to explore this sooner?

55% is the next winner because we all want to stay healthy and vigorous. Physical activities and healthy exercise include anything from the gym to personal landscaping, running or cycling to kite-boarding, hiking, skiing, swimming, and friendly or organized sports. We are the youngest generation of our age in all history. Naturally we want to stay active! Indeed traveling and vibrant physical health go excellently together.

38% also insist that cognitive vitality is key in retirement. "Learning, reading, educational experiences" …and these of course can be combined with other activities such as traveling and volunteering. Nourishing our mental wellbeing through good diet, healthy sleep patterns, physical activity, meditation/prayer, and a variety of new learnings and experiences, will help keep us vital and vibrant.

36% include the hands-on experiences of "Creating, cooking, writing, crafts and building things" as active and purposeful leisure. Consider my friend Peter ….

Peter was a high school principal long ago. He has continued traveling. He maintained physical, mental, spiritual wellbeing through a variety of activities from church to cottage, sailing to carpentry, family and friends, traveling near and far, and in his 90s remains fairly independent, still in the home overlooking the water where he has lived since the 1950s. I call him at times, and learn he's in the workshop building something for a great-grandchild. Peter has combined various aspects of leisure in a way that wonderfully exemplifies how we can enjoy long and healthy retirement living.

Personal Perspective. Review how we described leisure as something that is innately diversionary and refreshing from our normal course of duties. In our own lives, are we getting enough of this leisure? If yes, what's your secret and how can you share it to encourage others? If life or leisure feels stale, or something that used to be leisure has become a chore or duty, who would you speak with to open new possibilities, unlock this Rubik's cube of life, leisure, and refreshing re-creation? What is one step, perhaps an easy first-step, you can promise yourself today that will enrich your leisure?   And irrespective of anything it might cost, what are two or three life-changing ideas that would be the candle on your cake if you could enjoy even one of them in the next year or two? Ponder also, who else is part of this picture; who should be with you in these exploits?

"Plan to replace the things you enjoy doing in your business. … It is a paradox that the prospect of prolonged leisure and a perpetual holiday from work frequently does not fit the make-up of most successful business owners. For many… the transition into this new lifestyle may require having to learn how to enjoy leisure and still stay motivated. This is a good chance to look at the areas of your retirement life and decide what you want to accomplish in each area."   The Estate Planning Toolkit for Business Owners. CICA 2009.

QUESTION #4: Time could be a problem for me in retirement if:

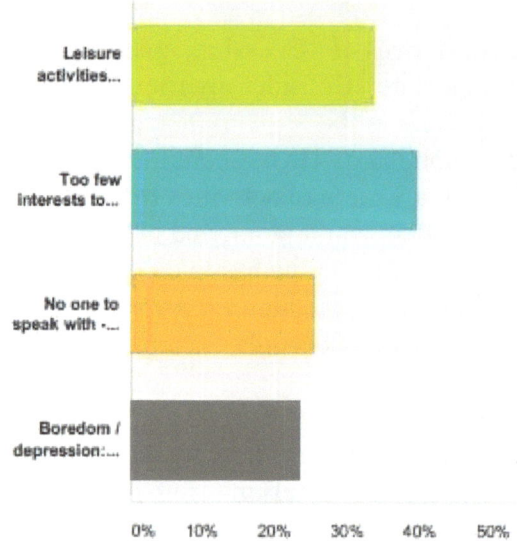

It's worth noting, one-third skipped this question, and yet **"time"** is one of our most vital areas to master in retirement lifestyles and aging. Fortunately people shared valuable and personal insights in the comments section, as well as in our individual interviews. Some of these interviews were with business owners or family where there is no intention of fully retiring.

39% say time could be a problem if they have "Too few interests to enjoy life throughout the year". This in itself justifies the purpose of our question. Refer to Q.3 where we explored the rich variety and renewing life-force of leisure …yet our strongest response here in Q.4 is the persistent worry that there won't be enough ways to entertain and keep ourselves interested.

25% express the worry of having "No one to speak with – not much to talk about." This is why we ended our Q.3 "personal perspective" on the topic of who will be with us, sharing in our life and leisure! Work has always been a key area of socialization. Take that away and we can become lonely, unhealthy, failing to thrive, unless or until we find new ways to connect and build social friendships.

24% also worry about "Boredom / depression, feeling 'life is over'." This is potentially catastrophic for members of our generation. What if business closes or a professional career gets "dislocated" before we're ready to retire? What if we fail to "practice for retirement" as I wrote a few years ago in "Jumping into the Retirement Wave"? We need to build an adaptive and refreshing lifestyle that prepares us for expanding interests in our future. Arts,  languages, travels, foods, sport, music, theatre, research, new-retirement careers/engagements – indeed anything that will keep our fires lit and our creative juices flowing.

The strangest response actually is 33% who say time could be a problem if "leisure activities start feeling like work." Story is told of a fellow who retired and left the office life …so now he tees off at 8 a.m. Monday to Friday. In this context is golf truly leisure? Recall "leisure" is something that is innately diversionary and refreshing from our normal course of duties. So has golf morphed into his new "work"? What other kinds of leisure activities do people turn into "work"? And if this happens, where will they find their true leisure?

We are a generation that will face these questions more than ever before. We weren't created to be idle; indeed we need purpose. That's where we can explore a "new retirement career" or creatively expand our leisure activities, even our volunteering. But if someone takes what used to be leisure and turns that into their new 8-5 routine they may soon find themselves struggling among the four pitfalls shown on our graph above.

Other comments on Q.4:
- If I take on too much
- If I end up working too much
- Lack of structure in daily activities
- Illness, impairments, chronic pain
- All good: new work, community activities
- Lots of interests; can't imagine being bored
- Not enough time to fit all I want to do ☺

Personal Perspective. How do you feel about "time" in life today? How would this compare with "time" in our childhood years? …in our teens? …when we were studying? …newly married? …raising young children? …in other key points of transition when we left one type of job for another? …when we opened or expanded our business? …when we've been away on vacations? How would you like a permanent vacation? …does this sound pleasant or repulsive? How comfortable is "time" right now at this age and in your activities today? What do you most want to change *(or what do you fear changing)* and why? Does this encourage you toward your goals for retirement, or what key pieces do you need in place to provide a good "fit" with retirement? If we blend this with earlier questions above, *and if money were no issue,* could you design a lifestyle that magnificently exemplifies how to enjoy "time"?

"Will your lifestyle remain the same (i.e., do you want to do more travelling, change where you live or provide financial help to your children or grandchildren? … Now that you are no longer the owner of a business, what are the emotional implications for you? How do you plan to spend the time that was previously occupied by your business?" Succession Planning Toolkit for Business Owners – leveraging your life's work. CICA 2006.

QUESTION #5: Key Role(s) when I retire: Who am I?

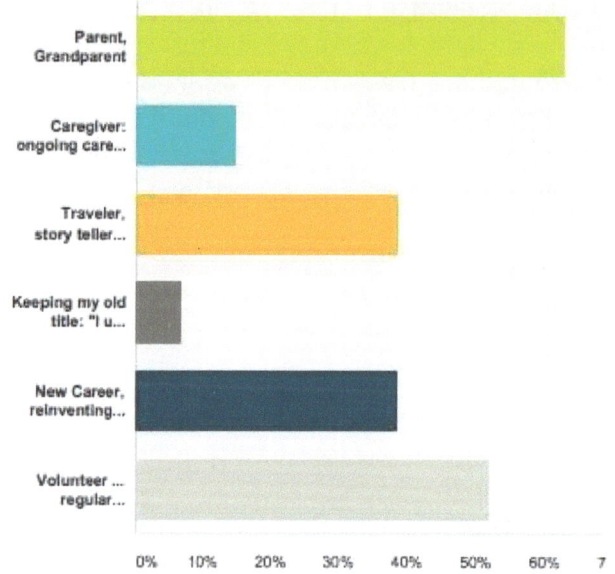

This is a vital area for everyone. Less than 1% passed over this question. In fact, we seem very enthusiastic about our future roles, and this is immensely encouraging. This means we might avoid what has been a darkening storm cloud on the horizon for many entering into retirement. "Storm" is no exaggeration for would you guess what age-group among men has the highest rate of suicide? Not teens, twenties, or mid-life: men in their 70s! Women often tended to build an identity larger than their labour, but men could identify so strongly with work-based roles and social connections that retirement could prove fatal. We all know some stories …so this is why we raise such a question here.

Time was, we'd ask a retired person, "Who are you – tell me about your life!" and we'd hear about their past career. JB described herself as a retired teacher. FB spoke of building from scratch into a sizable business. Another was "a railway man, to the day I die!" So many have described their life as WHO THEY USED TO BE …a retired minister, retired politician, retired social worker …"Oh I used to work at…", …you've heard it before. Great news: only **7% of business owners/executives expect they might fall into this trap**. Yet one wonders: did the fish know how it needed water until it was lifted out into the air? In the midst of our careers, even in later years, can we foresee how vital it is, and how to expand our roles and identity beyond our professional lives?

Strongest response at 63% identifies the enduring role in FAMILY. "Parent, Grandparent, Wife or Husband" …these roles are more compelling for lasting value and satisfaction than any other "title" on its own. Test this among our other questions. "Leisure" you said, will significantly include family. "Time" you said, could drag most if we're alone. Future "anxieties" may escalate without family support in areas of caregiving.

52% identify themselves with volunteer interests and contributing time and money to strengthen wider community in a thousand different ways. Fewer today are saying, "I paid my taxes; I did my duty!" People choose causes close to their hearts: all areas of health and research, environmental protection, hunger/homelessness, sports, business, coaching/mentoring, driving,

committee work, fund-raising, political action, faith and action, building homes, human rights, teaching languages, education/courses, or simply visiting the lonely. Our list could be endless. Wherever we contribute our time and experience to help others, we also support a strong sense of self and identity through retirement and senior years.

37% see a role as "Traveler, story-teller", sharing ideas and experiences from their travels near and far (see Q.3). People have shared with me a virtually unlimited reserve of stories from travels near and far. These travelers/story-tellers have brightened my own life, added colour and texture, sounds and sights, impressing on my heart the magnificence of our wonderful world. I've noticed though, if people don't take some time ahead to practice traveling – say a business owner who never leaves for extended breaks – future travels may elude them.

The traveler must have practiced how to get away, relieve stress, and expand their experience. **The traveler is also strengthening their business by encouraging a team who can manage on their own for a while …and if this fosters higher stability and business valuation, so much the better.**

Another 37% answer "Who am I" as "New career, reinventing myself in new work activities." I don't have to tell you, we're seeing more of this than ever. How many websites cater to exactly this type of lifestyle where we will combine our work/life balance in new ways and with new directions! Some resourceful websites to explore include: www.retiredbrains.com, www.Seniorpreneur.co.uk, www.Living55Plus.com. Nearer to us here: www.SilverGoldMagazine.ca and www.BM2B.ca *(boomer match to business)*. Many other sites too can reward your web search.

Caution raises a red flag where only 15% foresee a role in "caregiving" whether for parents, spouse, or others. No need for any gloom here for there are also silver-linings to grace these clouds. Did you know caregiving seems to increase our longevity …caregivers live longer! *(See links below.)* In fact caregiving can expand our sense of fun and social stimulation. Many will look back on their seasons together, grateful for precious memories and togetherness while caring for a loved one.

> Two quick resources on this:
> - http://www.boomertoboomeronline.ca/studies-suggest-that-family-caregivers-live-longer/
> - http://www.boomertoboomeronline.ca/caregivers-remember-to-have-a-good-time/

Ongoing care for others can alter life plans and levy punishing burdens on the unprepared. Without broader support from family or community, this too often is utterly exhausting. There are vital discussions to have today while everyone is well, to ensure future "sickness and health" will find optimal strength and resources for every need.

If parents are still living, will supporting their health care someday impact our retirement living? If temporary or lasting illness occurs for a spouse, partner, or for you and me, have we already labeled part of our wealth (or insurance) to buy needed care and support? Consider in-home nursing care, personal comfort and very-personal dignity! How will we care for the caregiver …to avoid burnout? If a child is permanently dependent (or becomes so) how will we balance roles of caregiving with our other life goals *(as above)* to enjoy all that we want to fulfill in our retirement living?

 **Personal Perspective**. Return to the graph above for insights that can turn up the lights in your future and protect the dreams you hold dear. Four of these responses can especially open doors to stronger identity roles and experiences we've been wanting to claim and enjoy. A fifth, caregiving, also holds rich opportunities to deepen life-value through illness or decline *…but carefully prepare and discuss these issues ahead or the result may not be "deepen" but "Deep-End!" Wouldn't we "depend" on having things together and arranged in advance?* Great caution too is #4, "keeping my old title" as it points to our past, forever invalidating our present. Ponder this and discuss with friends or someone close to you. How can we continue a vital, happy, and healthy sense of "self" through life's coming horizons?

Space for personal notes:

_____

_____

_____

_____

_____

_____

_____

QUESTION #6: Two Greatest Anxieties for Retirement …

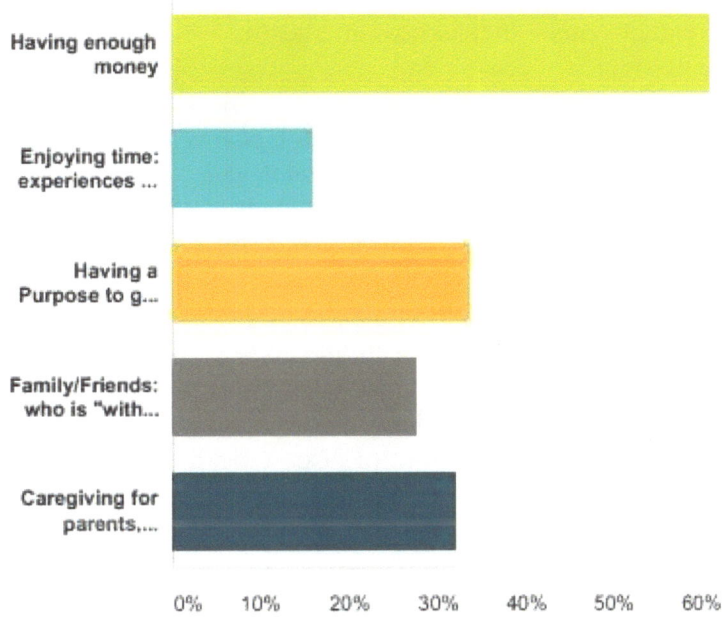

Look at how courageous we are to answer a question like this – *aside from 10% who passed over it* – so don't skip this! We want physical strength and mental wellbeing for a long and healthy retirement. We want enduring treasure to support our pleasures. One comment expresses the fear they'll never take time to slow down. Another is bravely "looking forward to embracing all of the above!"

61% of business owners and executives say their greatest concern is having enough money for retirement. Some context could help because I know one who feared he couldn't retire with $2 Million (after costs of selling business), while an employee felt new leadership was a good time to retire, with $95,000 in savings which was "more than enough".

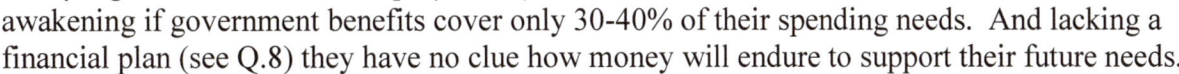

$2 Million isn't enough but $95,000 is surplus? Clearly these two have remarkably different experiences of money and lifestyle goals. As well, the employee may have a rude awakening if government benefits cover only 30-40% of their spending needs. And lacking a financial plan (see Q.8) they have no clue how money will endure to support their future needs.

The opposite puzzle is how to manage $2 Million after selling a business. Possibly this seller: (a) never before had $2M in their pockets, (b) lacks strategies against risks of low-return or high-volatility, and (c) feels stumped how to safeguard such capital for life-income and future estate (see Q.8).   Also, previous advisors may have dealt with smaller sums but new experience may be needed to protect and optimize this wealth for income and family estate value.

Just as the retiring employee (above) needs a financial plan, whoever sells a business has urgent reasons to own a comprehensive financial plan. This addresses all aspects of current and future wealth in and outside the business. It matches income-assets to lifestyle-expenses through early-, middle-, and later-retirement years – in 'sickness and health' – even for family estate (see Q.8).

As we'll see below in the OSC study by Brondesbury only 14% have a formal written financial plan to secure financial wellbeing in retirement. Usually, if there is a plan at all, pre-retirees have something in print to guide investments, while 25% of retirees have a plan that discusses their income. One ponders that if 61% say their greatest worry is having enough for retirement, the immediate answer should be, "Let's get a certified life and financial plan that can fully address all of this!"

34% express the second greatest worry, "Having a Purpose to get me moving each day." Some have no worries …they know what to do already, or they don't do much *and that's no place to be!* Have we touched on depression? Have we ever known someone who lacked vigour or "luminosity" as Dr. Johnson calls it in "What Color Is Your Retirement?" This is vital to our health and wellness, which isn't just an absence of disease but a well formed identity, activity, and purpose that gets us moving each day. If you're experiencing uncertainty here review Q.2 on creatively expanding life's purpose and significance.

Caregiving for parents, spouse, grand/children is here at 32%. Sometimes a survey doesn't just measure response but also helps develop our perspective. In Q.5 just 15% saw caregiving as a future role but Q.6 shows twice as many with caregiving as a major anxiety. In Q.5 we found a silver-lining in caregiving, but yes it matters greatly if there's help from family and community to carry the burden. Disability is no respecter of age or status; it can hit any of us in our 90s, 80s, even our 50s, and some have been so since childhood. The impact could mean weeks, seasons, or years of care, from minor expense and temporary burdens to one of your most compelling financial and daily priorities.

Don't face this alone! Can family help? What outside resources have you identified? Did you arrange insurance-funding or other savings? As I've served families and seniors in two careers for nearly four decades I assure you we can combine family, financial, and community resources in a wholesome plan that supports each person, giving and/or receiving care.

27% reflect our fears that society has become so solitary and disjointed, asking, "Who is with me to share life?" How many fingers must you use to count the friends who would join

you on a trip to Paris, or an RV trip to Palm Springs, or settle in with you for a week after returning from hospital? Many are fortunate with such a spouse, friend, or child, but today we have more singles than ever! More life-long singles than ever!

So the question remains, "Who is with me to share life?" One person told me after selling the last of his business three years ago, "My wife died of cancer, and I like to travel; but when I see something beautiful I want to turn around and share this experience …but no one is there!"

As a financial and retirement coach I ponder the stories and concerns people have been sharing with me for many years. Looking ahead we can naturally expect to face some of these concerns in our own lives.

To reduce our worries and face the future with confidence, we can draw some clear conclusions. First is the value of preparing and possessing a clear, certified financial plan, showing how our wealth can abundantly support our opportunities, needs, and comforts (see Q.8). Second is to build our lifestyle for purpose and personal reward in each and every season (see Q.2). Third, we realize seasons can come when time or money must support us or other dear ones through a season of frailty. Fourth, nurture family and friends, even expand our relationships, because as we live long and healthy, our future friends may be much younger than we are! Fifth, let's encourage the 16% fearing they have too few ways to truly enjoy their time (see Q.4). Life is a rich gift each day that, before it slips away, deserves our best creativity and sharing, in the hope that all can enjoy the journey!

Personal Perspective. Remember what I said on page 3 about polls, like peering down to the mountain tops from 35,000 feet …but our focus here is really about you, me, and our own personal mountain. If you look back at the graph would you find one or more areas where your worry is 7 or above on a scale of 1-10? Is it about money? …about purpose to give our days meaning? …about the time when "sickness and health" means caring for another? …or being the focus of another's care? …is it about the people you want in life to enjoy social contact and friendship? Forget everyone else for a few minutes here; what are your key areas? Which is your #1 priority, that if we fill this gap it can invigorate your view of retiring?

Space for personal notes:

QUESTION #7: To secure Savings for Retirement I can …

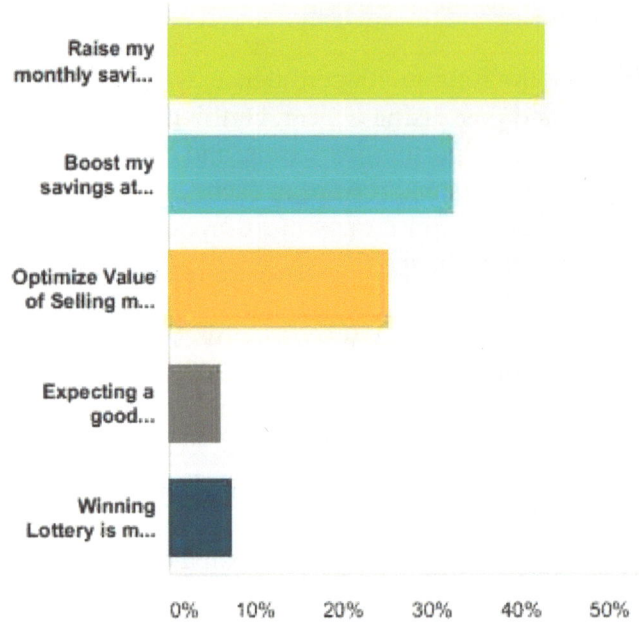

As we saw in Q.6, we have 61% of business owners and executives saying they're already afraid that their savings are insufficient to afford their real retirement dreams. Here in Q.7 we want to answer how we'll fill this gap. We don't want to be like this monopoly man...

43% say they can raise their monthly savings immediately by at least 5%. I wonder, after completing the survey, have they done so? Their gap still persists unless they've taken this action, so it's something to ponder for ourselves.

Easier for some, 32% say they will increase their savings at least 10% …allowing six to twelve months to prepare for this commitment. In fact it's proven, as I discuss elsewhere, that people are more able to make a future commitment than a current one, especially where it involves money. And you'd suppose maybe they won't keep that future commitment, yet a great many do. And the ones who do win!

See the two smaller responses in the graph above. **7% say their only hope is winning a lottery** *(and if you win a lottery, your best hope of keeping that money is in what I shared in chapter 4 of A Lifetime of Wealth – and How Not To Lose It)*. **6% feel safe in "expecting a good inheritance"** …and on this theme see chapter 3 in that book as we link the DNA of your family's values into guarding value you may inherit from them. The key theme of inherited wealth or windfalls comes down to how you shape, articulate, and activate your inner values around money. Absent that lesson – *without such a process* – there's nearly a 100% chance of losing much or all of the wealth you've found.

Vital of course for business owners – even executives in such firms – would be **"Optimizing Value of Selling my Business."** We know that many of the businesses in our region – indeed over 500,000 businesses in Canada, 2 Million in the U.K., 5 Million in the U.S.A. – are destined to successfully transition (or close) in roughly the next 5 years. We hear that 80% of them haven't the team or planning process to optimize their potential sale value. Wouldn't a business and its key people want to tap into this? Wouldn't an executive consider the potential rewards of locking-in such value, or even purchase and then optimize enterprise value in their own right?

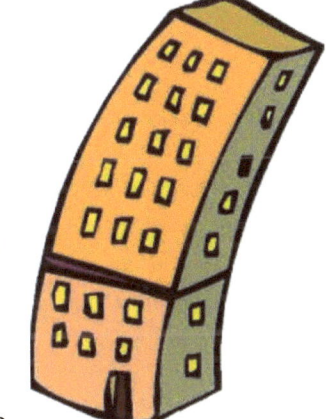

Vast sums are being left on the table, particularly for SME (small and mid-sized businesses) throughout our world's democracies. Aside from personal service businesses *whose value may depend intimately on today's owner,* consider the possibilities right here where we live! How many SMEs will close instead of selling, will limp into an inventory sale for lack of strategic partners, or take an offer instead of engaging a more lucrative exit?

25% of owner/executives responded that optimizing value of their business could help their financial resources for retirement. Can we better explore and mobilize this option? Have you discussed and moved this ahead with your strategic planning team?

Key within such a "stewardship team" are your accounting firm, certified financial advisor, insurance and estate advisors, business attorney, and selected business consultants. Some sites you might explore to focus your consultation goals are noted below, as well as a couple of books. What professional competencies and team members could best combine to expand your enterprise, community value, and lucrative exit?

- http://www.light-core.com/
- http://www.dougsunlimited.com/
- http://www.theplatinumyears.com/
- http://www.warrenbdc.com/.

- John Mill, <u>Hire Your Buyer</u>.
- Thomas William Deans, <u>Every Family's Business</u>.
- Jack Beauregard, <u>Finding Your New Owner</u>.

Personal Perspective. Don't go broke. Revisit the above graph, select one or two bits there and also write in your own ideas to build such financial security that you'll never be able to spend it all. What would happen, or what would it feel like if your wealth kept expanding even in retirement? Would it eliminate worries? Would it open more opportunities? Could you do more for family? …increase your footprint through philanthropy? Would your heart swell with gratitude, would your life feel bigger somehow, when you've found how to reliably expand your financial wellbeing?

"Treat yourself as an employee when it comes to your retirement plan and insist that your business provide for you when you decide to leave. Don't…assume your nest egg will come (from) proceeds of the business sale or transfer. As a business owner, you have the decision-making ability to create a retirement plan for your employees (which includes you). …separate your needs as a business owner from your needs as an individual who is trying to plan financially for the future." The Estate Planning Toolkit for Business Owners. CICA 2009.

"If you are a business owner over 50, you WILL leave your business someday. You only have two choices: plan for it on your own terms, or let others plan it for you. Which sounds better to you?" Jack Beauregard.

Space for personal notes:

_____

_____

_____

_____

_____

QUESTION #8: Planning for the Life I Want …

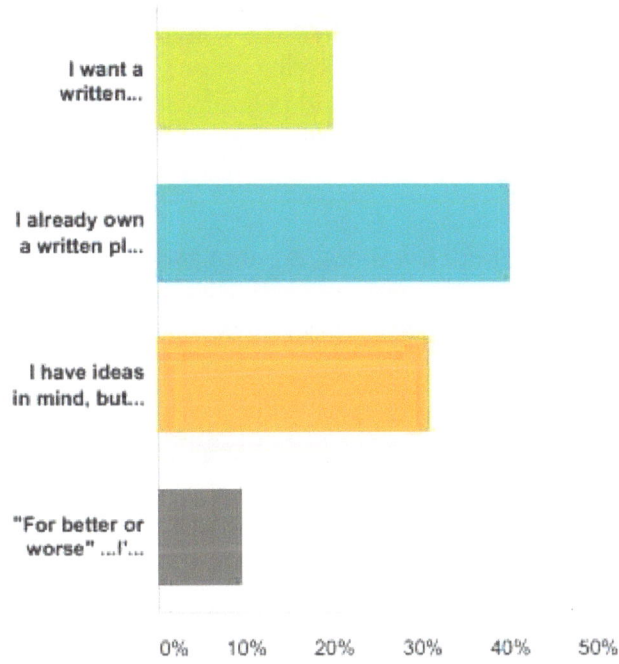

Please don't take it wrongly if I ask what your future is worth. If you were in a working group to feed the world's hungry children you'd go into extensive coordination and planning. If you were helping raise the next bid for the Olympics you'd certainly have an extended plan. If we were serving as a disaster relief team after a major catastrophe – think Haiti, or Nepal – designing and working the plan would be vital. In fact, for your business and career you've already been planning and achieving certain targets, so this isn't so new, is it?

Yet when it comes to 20, 30, 40 years of retirement most people have given it less planning than for last year's summer holidays. "It will take care of itself" is a phrase sometimes heard. **9% in our survey said, "For better or worse I'll accept whatever comes."**   One guess …how does that work out?

40% say, "I already own a "written financial plan guiding life and security to age 90/95+." If we believe that, we'd also say every lawyer has a Will, right? Wrong! Pull out your plan, hold it in your hands, see where it's been published in the past three to five years and how it speaks to your assets, risks, growth, retirement date, and lifestyle horizons through ages 60 to 75, 75 to 86, and 87 to 95+. Is this how your plan appears? …no? *…or were you saying you have an investment plan showing some assets? This isn't the same thing at all!   In the Brondesbury/OSC study we'll see that **only 14% have written financial***

plans. Among retirees 25% have some kind of planning but even these usually fail to address eventual needs that arise with Lifestyle, Health / Illness, Family emergencies, and final Estate.

Absolutely it's worthwhile owning a certified financial plan and review this every 6 to 12 months so you can freely discuss your future in living colour. You describe your goals and values in enjoying life! We verify investment and planning mandates to secure your personal dreams, goals, and lifestyles through all the seasons ahead. *(See Q.9, how many horizons in your future?)*

20% in our survey say they want such a financial plan but they've never seen or owned one. They possibly don't even know what to expect! These are people I'd like to meet today *and every day* because building these plans is exactly what our certifications and experience equip us to offer. In 2013 *(see <u>A Lifetime of Wealth – And How Not To Lose It</u>, pages 124-125)* I shared two approaches we can combine simultaneously: a formal process of four main steps, and an experiential process that vividly aligns financial resources with your personal life goals.

Another 31% would also fit nicely into my calendar. These are people who answered, **"I have ideas in mind but no real plan; cannot afford it now."** Truth is, if you can share with me the ideas you have in mind, and we take these as your values for retirement

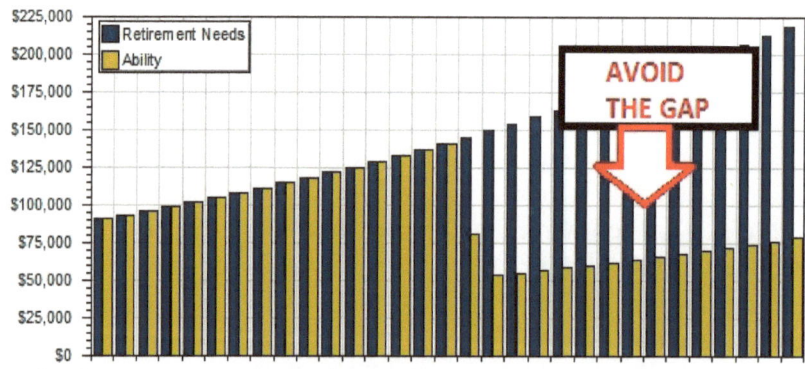

living, we'll align your savings and other resources into a strategic plan for your success.

Cost? You choose! Some clients opt to pay a fee and then implement the results themselves. Others have us implement the financial plan and investments so we can waive further fees. This plan needn't take any money out of your pocket. Indeed it's overwhelmingly proven that people of equal means and circumstances end up with far more wealth by owning a certified financial plan, compared to those who lack such a plan.

Personal Perspective. You could set the above aside for a moment and consider other areas of life. How do you run your business, your home, vacations, car repairs, debts, mortgages, even meals and exercise? Do you plan for any of these? …of course you do! Where you don't have a plan, would it work better if you did? Wouldn't you agree it makes sense, that bringing all your resources into a wholesome financial plan *(now to age 95+)* would bring greater clarity, confidence, certainty, and comfort for years and seasons to come? If it costs a little time now and periodic reviews along the way would this plan still have merit? If there's an invoice or if it's marked PAID by the way we implement your plan, would this too hold value for you?

If 85% or more are lacking a sufficient plan for the future, what's the next logical step? Hanging in the balance is life, career and business, and how you want to transition these into your retirement dreams and your enduring comfort. Are you ready for a certified plan in which we can map out the future you choose?

Timing and Planning: *"...the owner does not always have control over timing of the sale or transfer of ...the business. Everything from external market conditions to locating a willing buyer can delay retirement until the owner can fully realize its value. ... Though they run successful businesses and are used to making business plans, few business owners take the same care in planning their own futures. Less than two out of five even have a succession or retirement plan in place to follow the sale of their business. ...the owner has not often thought about 'life after business'."* The Estate Planning Toolkit for Business Owners. CICA 2009.

Space for personal notes:

QUESTION #9: How many Horizons for Retirement?

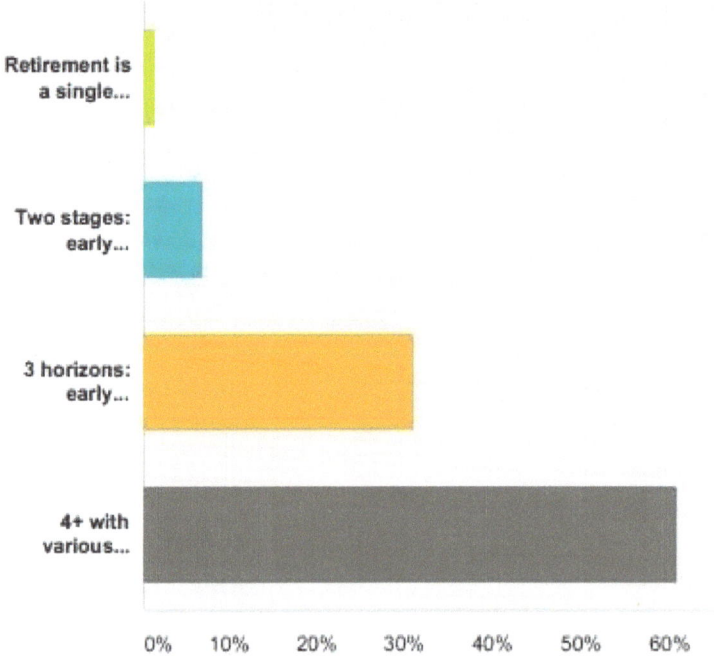

Here was my "Mount Everest" experience when I received the results and tested them in our personal interviews. This graph would totally shock how financial planning is done today.

A typical financial plan – if one even has such a plan – looks generally like a straight line or what I've referred to as the "flat-line" (seen in the lower blue area below) because it suggests people live just one-horizon, a single period of life from retirement to death, in which they spend a fixed sum of money each month and their needs never vary. Hardly likely! And you agree! **1.35% of respondents said this is how they see their future**. Maybe due to life-threatening illness? Or poverty *(not in our sample)*? Or as one said, "I'll retire to a box" meaning he intends to keep working for the sheer love and pleasure of it, so the closest answer he could give here is a "single" period or horizon. No one else wants this flat-line!

Just 6.76% see the future as two horizons, early activities and travels, followed by declining health. Some of these may have illness, or short-lived families. Some may feel there's just not enough money, or a shortage of dreams and thrills to fuel a long life.

92% say they expect to experience three or four horizons after their *(intial?)* **retirement**. This is the red portion shown here noted as "real life spending", what I call the life-horizons-line. Some will downsize a career, or start-up a new

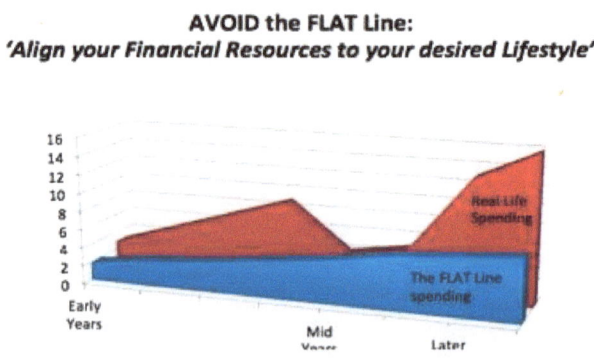

business, migrate responsibilities to other staff, or pick up major volunteer activities – and this can extend into our 70s, 80s, and beyond depending on our desire and opportunities. We certainly expect to travel actively: we'll explore and expand leisure activities as we've already seen in Q.3. One or more seasons may be touched by caring for a loved one – or indeed being convalesced ourselves. Some will study on-line and others will attend courses (Q.3).

Physical abilities will also change. I've described elsewhere how early retirement can present the greatest opportunities for active living and travel *(you clearly agree)* so we can expand our lifestyle budget in this first period. Mid-retirement can become more sedentary, less travel, more pictures and stories of places we used to visit and people we met along the way. If given long life, we eventually need more personal support. And how fast are those costs rising!?! **WILL YOUR FINANCIAL PLAN secure the resources for each of these horizons of retirement and senior living?** (see Q.8).

For myself, I see continuing an early-retirement career, which in my case means continuing my service as today but on fewer hours, so I also expand other experiences of travel, art, volunteer and physical activities, and cherishing our family. My 2nd horizon comes when I leave working completely – perhaps age 75 or whenever we cancel my licences and registrations to practice as I do today. My 3rd horizon likely begins about the time age creeps up and my driver's licence goes, suggesting capacities decrease and personal needs increase. My 4th horizon is how I describe what happens in my estate planning for my wife, children, and extended family, as well as the wider footprint of our philanthropic goals.

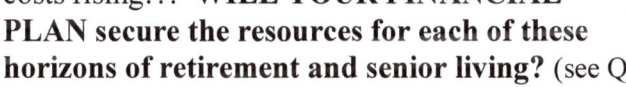

Personal Perspective. Take a moment now for yourself. Put a few bullet-points on paper, or start to envision the movie of your future and how it should play out, in your own terms. How many horizons do you see? What events may punctuate the beginnings and changes of such seasons? If we had a plan to expand and extend your life, health, and financial resources, how can this widen your retirement living?

We answer only to ourselves – even while discussing with friends and family – as we shape and direct our future. Have you been trapped assuming life and money is a "flat-line" in retirement? How could you expand your imagination to ramp up retirement, live large and wonderfully, create and capture your bucket lists?

Yet living long may lead sooner or later to declining strength and that's where we don't want to be leaving health bills to our children. *Sad where children's retirement savings get tapped for parents' care!* No point grumbling if we never made plans. No use complaining if business declines when markets shift or currencies go "looney", or political changes turn for the worse. We answer only to ourselves, so take courage and take charge now!

Those who want a resilient future will want to ensure free and flexible resources for life's future horizons. This is where you get to script, direct, and "star" in your own movie … all documented in your CERTIFIED LIFE AND FINANCIAL PLAN.

Also see:
- o Developing lifestyles: Rick Bava, <u>In Search of the Baby Boomer Generation</u>.
- o On business and family estate: Thomas William Deans, <u>Willing Wisdom</u>.

"Failing to get the professional help you need could be the most significant factor in not achieving your financial goals. … Remember: an effective financial advisor will spend the time to get to know you … (and) can have a significant impact on the outcome of your financial plan. Taking the time to select the right individual helps ensure you have an effective partner in managing your future."
Succession Planning Toolkit for Business Owners – leveraging your life's work. CICA 2006.

Space for personal notes:

_____

_____

_____

_____

_____

_____

SECTION #10: REVIEW OF WIDER POLLS AND STUDIES

Other public studies intersect dynamically with our discussion. They generally touch a wider range of age, stage, income, and occupation with commentary shaped by sponsors who paid the bill. As I shared in the opening introduction, **these polls are like a wider "MAP."** Where I want to focus is a sign that says, **"YOU ARE HERE".**

If big national studies were key to your business, you'd be on their mailing list – subscribed and waiting for the big release. But probably you've missed many of these studies because you're so busy in your career and business, and at most got a quick glimpse in the newspaper or on TV.

Let's dive into a few of these studies to glean what insights we can find. It's a bit like chatting with other travelers at the mountaintop. What are they seeing? What immediate challenges do they forecast? What conclusions could arise from their research?   And remember as I said earlier, **what matters for you isn't about others but the impact on your personal journey!**

Manulife / Ipsos Reid. Health and Wellness Study, 2014.

This study found major illness in our workforce. 50% of workers report mental health issues and a leading cause is financial stress. Only 40% of businesses offer retirement savings plans; of these, most offer little or no planning to advise when and how staff may be able to safely retire. Proposed solution is 3-fold for the employer that wants a healthy and profitable team now and for the future: retirement savings plan, debt-planning, and access to a reliable financial planner.

This discussion revealed that staff benefiting from these strategies will more likely experience work as a locus of lifelong learning and increasing opportunity – attitudes we can nurture even into retirement. The message here for any size of business is that financial planning through the workplace will pay significant dividends in bottom-line profits. Employees will be better able to adapt to life's pressures pre- and post-retirement. Business valuation too will trend higher, of clear benefit to the intending "seller" as well as to the future of this enterprise and its community.

2014 CAP Member Survey.

On a similar theme this study sponsored mainly by three insurers acknowledges that, in existing "capital accumulation plans" *(group retirement)*, "it's hard to get plan members to save enough money, to spend time ...planning for retirement and to understand (how) to be successful." It asks further, **"what happens when employees reach their planned retirement age but don't have enough money to retire?"**

In groups that host such savings, 50% of employees feel plans will be sufficient to help them retire. Caution though; they also believe they're averaging 12.9 % annual returns. Three major risks loom for the future of these employers: (1) when employees realize savings are inadequate when they want to retire, (2) potential of class-action suits when many face such disappointment simultaneously *(eg. Nortel pension)*, and (3) employer's reputation when such events turn sour.

Consider your competition. 87% of participating employers believe they have a responsibility to help employees prepare for retirement. 92% say it's valuable to their organization to help staff prepare for an adequate retirement income.

Further lessons we can draw from this: (1) help staff understand the value of increasing their deposits, (2) encourage participation by mandatory enrollment or competitive employer-matching to staff contributions, (3) design the plan to prevent or discourage pre-retirement withdrawals, (4) help staff realize that "default" portfolio options can be so conservative as to achieve zero growth, (5) include access to professional financial planning to enhance success in employee wealth-management *and to reduce potential liability to the employer*, and (6) plan also for the eventual "de-accumulation" from savings into withdrawals for life-long income.

Financial Executives Intl (FEI). Are Your Pension Funds Being Managed?

Focus in this 2015 study here is to de-risk pension arrangements. Employers already know that traditional Defined Benefit Pensions carry risk for investment, fiduciary care, and lengthening lifespans. Some risks shift to employees in DC plans and group RRSPs. FEI offers a picture here to demonstrate the shocking impact of timing (retirement) on pension income.

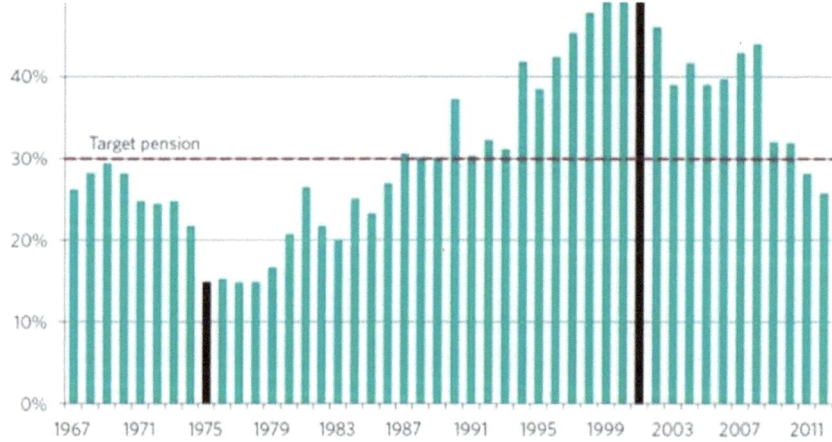

Adjusting to 1975 dollars or thinking of the amount of "lifestyle" one can buy, the identical person retiring in 2001 could afford a 3-times higher lifestyle compared to retiring in 1975. But retiring in 2015, they'd be locking in a 40% reduced standard of living. No wonder other statistics show such high worry about money! Non-voluntary (forced) early retirements *or delays due to inadequate savings* will hurt business, families, and wider community interests.

Key areas in this discussion include: (1) investment risks, (2) pension liabilities and solvency, (3) increasing lifespans requiring longer pay-outs, and (4) risks of administration and governance.

De-risking strategies include: (1) improved governance, (2) matching investment assets to long-term liabilities, (3) insuring risks of longevity, and (4) other amendments to pension design.

Ponder if you can think of an employer with rich pension obligations but a severe shortfall of funding. A few names might come to mind from the news. A theme is opening up in our discussion, revealing the benefits of retirement planning that truly impacts all levels of the business, owners, staff and families, today and future. What FEI clarifies is the danger of using old and outdated strategies in view of impending future liabilities that can impact any business, whether large or small.

Sun Life / Ipsos Reid. Canadian Unretirement Index Report.

"Unretirement" is here defined as "the growing trend away from early retirement – by choice or economic necessity – and towards continued work past the traditional retirement age of 65." 2015 is the first time this report has shown a majority plan to work beyond 65, and of these 59% sadly admit their situation is forced by financial need.

81% feel they'd be fine covering "basic living expenses" but they want more! Only 11% or one out of ten declare being "very satisfied" – 33% "somewhat satisfied" – with retirement savings. If they knew the costs and inflation that hit travel, medical, and other family needs, perhaps the "satisfied" would be an even smaller minority.

70% see a clouded future, fearing they could outlive their savings. Only a third say they have some kind of financial advisor. One out of five say they have a written plan.

Key worries for this group repeat what we've seen above: debt and housing costs, investment losses, reduced benefits in group retirement plans, and a persistent fear that the future is less abundant than advertised.

Turning to those already retired, the study offers some hope as 63% of retirees are "very" or "somewhat satisfied" with the life currently secured with their savings. Nearly half however worry their financial and personal wellbeing will drop as they age. With 37% unsatisfied and 30% more who foresee future difficulties, the study suggests two-thirds are afraid for their future.

Where 100 measures optimism for a perfect retirement, Sun Life Unretirement Index for 2015 scores poorly at **46**. These people can include you and me, our families, our staff, and our neighbours. They affect our business in terms of profits and growth, valuation, sale, and/or succession. It's the old story, how can we get what we want unless we help others get what they want! Business value and retirement readiness will prove inextricably linked.

BRONDESBURY GROUP – for the Ontario Securities Commission: FINANCIAL LIFE STAGES OF OLDER CANADIANS.

Released in the spring of 2015 this report finds that most people over 50 and in retirement have only an informal personal approach to financial planning and this is accompanied by a limited understanding of the kinds of future expenses that will arise as time unfolds.

Furthermore, we learn that at least 60% ultimately face unexpected events that threaten their financial and total wellbeing. This factor is so strong (and often multiple in nature) that it seems irresponsible for any financial plan to project the future without allowing for unknown risks and disappointments, especially along the following lines:

- Forced early retirement, often due to poor health,
- Need to support others such as parents and/or children,
- Unexpected longevity *(>85 is our fastest growing age group)*,
- Rise of chronic illness and costs of care with advancing age,
- Permanent investment losses,
- Fraud.

It's worth pondering the opening of a question in this study: "Sometimes 'big' things happen that make it very difficult... We aren't just talking about having a hard time... We are talking about unexpected things that happen that take up a lot of your money." Those "big" things hit most homes and yet appear in very few of today's financial plans.

This study chastises financial planners as a group for overwhelmingly failing to address health management and accelerating costs. We should realize as a certainty that the future will unfold in ways we cannot see today, and we need to build this into the context and design of our plans. Not knowing which events *or how many* could put our future at risk, certified planning can provide buffers, contingencies, and ongoing reviews to avoid such threats to our personal and financial safety. *(See Q.9 above: poverty is not among our desired future horizons.)*

Under the surface is a theme that seniors often adjust to their circumstances and find satisfaction within their means. *(We could say, money forces boundaries and people learn to accept them.)* The **sting** lies in not knowing how long we'll live. Satisfaction today may disguise tomorrow's want and vulnerability. If money lasts to 85, yet life continues to 95, this can prove devastating.

"Advice on health preparation is comparatively scarce among financial planners, while nothing is more common than advising on risk and return of investments". "There needs to be more planning for health management ... underestimated as a source of potential financial disruption."

"Outliving my/our money" is a top worry among pre- and post-retirees who give this any thought. Of sixteen areas where people express worry, every one touches on the danger of outliving our money.

Lessons and implications for "Your Business, Your Retirement" repeat what we have drawn out of other studies above.

McKinsey & Company. Building on Canada's Strong Retirement Readiness.

McKinsey surveys larger groups, illustrating many areas of retirement readiness from year to year. In 2012 they reported, "the majority of Canadian households are well-prepared and on track to maintain their standard of living in retirement. Many will also have the opportunity to leave an inheritance. However, close to a quarter …are not on track to generate a retirement income sufficient to maintain their standard of living when they move out of the workforce."

In Feb. 2015 they specified that only 17% of households seem destined to fall short of reasonable income replacement in retirement, and 33% while marginally safe are spending below their retirement goals. In sum, nearly one-fifth could be destined for poverty, and one-third would fall below the lifestyle they desired and intended.

Strong points from McKinsey's research and interpretation include:

- Recent trend is to delay retiring by a year or more, offering more time to save, less time to spend, thus enhancing retirement readiness scores.

- Low-income homes with little or no access to employer-based pensions fare poorly here. Targeting 80% income-replacement *as earlier income was so low* government benefits are a main pillar of their future security. Pension and personal savings are likely very low. If owning a home was also out of reach, such equity too is unavailable. Further issue arises if even modest pension causes claw-back of government benefits.

- Middle- to higher-income households who fall short may satisfy the shortfall through home ownership and other assets. Proposing 30% or more of home equity to maintain retirement income, "readiness" approaches 100% *…defined as two-thirds of former income*. There are a number of ways one can unlock value of a house to gain income for senior living.

- People who contribute > 5% to employer-based retirement savings plans are also in a stronger position for retirement. Yet 11% contribute less. 31% in a plan contribute nothing.

- 60% across all income bands *($10K to $250K per year)* worry at "not having enough money for retirement" and McKinsey poses a "perception gap" as people over-estimate retirement spending patterns. They say only 14% of homes increase spending, while 53% choose to spend less. 33% are unable to satisfy their desired spending.

Readers could be building two lines of thought with this study: (1) Where does this impact our own lifestyle goals? (2) For staff who are financially more vulnerable, what are the duties and opportunities for business to strengthen their employees' retirement readiness?

- In our own situation, consider your comfort if we define readiness as "the standard of living (you can) afford in retirement relative to peak working life standard of living". If retirement gives you 60-67% of your work-life income, will this sustain the life you want to be enjoying? Maybe the house is paid, kids are launched, debts are clear. And even if that's all true, weren't there new opportunities and experiences you wanted to invest in and enjoy as the rewards of your career?   So consider honestly, do you see yourself in the 14% who can easily increase spending? Would you, like the 50%, be happy to fit your life to a more restricted income? Where and how large is the gap *(see p.34)* we want to repair so you can avoid having to constrain lifestyle due to failed saving or planning?

- Risks I find unreported in McKinsey include a potential "bubble" of housing values *(especially if one includes home equity for spending)*; accelerating pharmaceuticals and healthcare costs; volatility and/or low-returns experienced in personal and pension-based savings. McKinsey also says little of the 67% who say illness, job-loss, other calamities have set back their retirement security. Such dominant factors from Brondesbury's research should/would strengthen our approach to retirement readiness.

- McKinsey seems silent too on the value of helping employees access financial planning. Elsewhere it's clear that people contribute more, participate more, see stronger results where they have professional support and guidance. McKinsey could encourage higher participation in employee savings through access to professional financial guidance.

- Does having a large sample give stronger results? McKinsey's study for the Feb. 2015 release includes 9,000 aged 25 to 65 and 3,000 retired households. It's a wide sample, but clearly four generations – and retirees themselves can be distinguished in a number of sub-groups. However large a study may be, generalizations can be misleading and confusing. And while the study encourages broad strategies for retirement readiness, it lacks clarity for the owner/executive seeking their retirement goals.

People can raise a fundamental question of any and all such studies: "Are we eager to retire on just two-thirds of our career income? Haven't we a bucket-list of travel and other lifestyle choices to enjoy, plus in some later horizon the vital costs of personal dignity and lasting comfort? What personal decisions would we make to define our goals and expand our retirement readiness?"

CONCLUSIONS AND GOING FORWARD

I'm grateful as we've come to this point together. I began this study due to witnessing a continuing crisis that touches our businesses, careers, retirement, and estate planning.

I've seen businesses close that could have fetched a reasonable value and provided retirement funds to the seller, and a new horizon and opportunity to buyer, staff, and community.

Some in management slackened the pace as they hoped to buy the business – but didn't want to drive up the value (price) until after their succession.

I've heard business owners describe their role, identity, and lifestyle in a business and they regret an approaching sale or succession. Even a competitive offer to purchase may fail when the business owner is unsure how to satisfy personal needs for money, time, purpose, identity, or socialization.

Look over the past 5, 10, 20 years and we see businesses have closed – some well but others unnecessarily. Were they coasting? Was there a lack of focus on the key drivers for successful growth? Did a key person's death or illness result in financial loss and jeopardy to employees, customers, and wider community?

As well, are some people afraid retirement will accelerate their aging, decline, and death? Would retiring mean losing self-identity and role in community? Were owners waiting to learn if their children really want to be involved? What are the personal worries around "money" (see Q.1, Q.6, and Q.7) …getting enough of it; even the fear of outliving it?

My conclusions fit the following questions. Have you a "stewardship team" of advisors, family, and others who help guide your journey to the destination you want? Have you a truly Certified Financial Plan that embraces all aspects of life and wealth today, business and family, retirement lifestyle, and estate planning? Such a planning process offers the full 360° I promised on page 3, knowing that all stakeholders *(in life, business, and community)* can be stronger as a result.

Your own conclusions as reader are vital. You bring individual experience, passion, and wishes to this work. Here you can learn, grow, and adjust habits to achieve desired results. As we can focus and help you master your personal journey in business and retirement planning, how soon can we speak together?

Have you spent time on the mountain? Have you begun a 360° view of your business, your retirement? In your life today what areas are "green"? What areas mark caution? And if you recognize time-bombs or stop-lights on your path, are you ready for us to help **turn the lights in your favour**?

More resources in retirement planning:

Richard P. Johnson, Ph.D.   The New Retirement. Discovering your Dream. 2001. P.1-2.

"The 'new retirement' is not an ending, it's a new beginning, the start of a new life journey of vastly expanded proportion."

"The old retirement model produced idle busyness, self-forfeiture, powerlessness, and reliance on others; the new retirement fosters life enrichment, healthy self-ownership, transformation, and creative self-reliance." Also the new retirement "encourages physical wellness, a healthy self-esteem, an attitude of mentorship, and a posture of involvement." And "the new retirement enhances relationships with new communication, new cohesion, and new adaptive freshness."

* The book introduces his "**Life Options Profile**™" bringing together 15 key factors in life experience that can help prepare or hinder a successful retirement. As a base for retirement coaching the LOP reveals how prepared we are today in terms of achieving our own goals and dreams for retirement, as well as how we compare with averages in the wider population. This opens areas to discuss and strengthen prior to leaving business/career and launching retirement.

Richard P. Johnson, Ph.D.   What Color is your Retirement? The LifeOptions guidebook to discover, plan and live your retirement dream. 2006. P.169.

"Retirement is supposed to be a challenging stage of life. … Where there was strength, determination now appears. Where speed once carried the day, now thoughtful understanding wins it. Where once sensory sharpness gave us an edge, now patience and wisdom provide us with sustaining power. Your retirement is like your life…. Invest little and receive little … invest a lot and find your life."

"Will retirement remain what it has been for so many before you, a time for the pursuit of diversion, or will a new retirement emerge when and where people seek to become ever more who they truly are … filled with vitality of mind, verve of spirit and vigor of passion? You will craft your own retirement, but you will also be setting the stage for generations behind you."

* This book introduces his "**Retirement Success Profile**™", a remarkably effective process available in retirement coaching to strengthen our retirement-preparedness in six key areas of life: (i) career and work, (ii) health and wellness, (iii) finances and insurance, (iv) family and relationships, (v) leisure and social, (vi) personal development. RSP results immediately illustrate our retirement readiness in terms of red-, amber-, green-light. Green shows readiness. Amber reveals areas to examine and strengthen if possible. Red-light marks hazards we can address to create for ourselves a stronger, happier, more satisfying future.

Expanding on themes we've opened here in Your Business, Your Retirement I am continuing interviews with people like yourself so we can expand and deepen lessons we have opened here. As well, watch for my next book due in 2016, Pathways to a New Retirement.

100% of the proceeds of this publication and all this author's books and website are contributed to the following community initiatives and resources:

The Early and Lifelong Nutrition Fund
hosted in the Burlington Community Foundation
and also in the Oakville Community Foundation

The Indigenous Sharing and Learning Centre
Laurentian University, Sudbury, Ontario

Other human relief and development services globally.

Thank you for enjoying, sharing, and supporting these resources for stronger homes and families, business and communities, and safer futures for your retirement and family.

Yours gratefully,

Brian Weatherdon

Certified Financial Planner, Certified Retirement Coach.
Brian@SovereignWealth.ca
905-637-3500 ext. 223

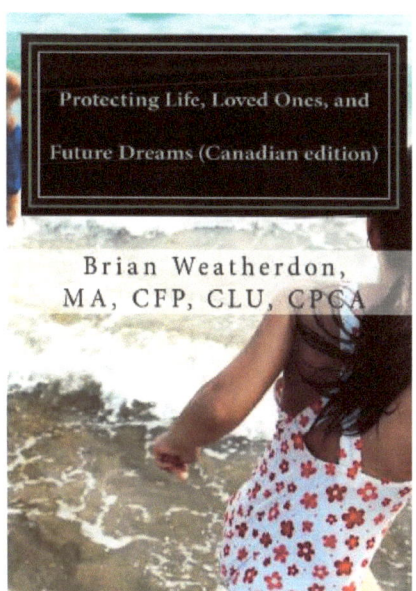

www.ingramcontent.com/pod-product-compliance
Lightning Source LLC
Chambersburg PA
CBHW050405180526
45159CB00005B/2163